GW00726175

Golden Moments

for busy teachers

Jenny Mosley

Published by:
Positive Press Ltd
28A Gloucester Road
Trowbridge
Wiltshire BA14 OAA
ISBN 0-9540585-2-6

First published 2003
© Positive Press Ltd
Text © Jenny Mosley
Design by Jeanne Powell

Golden Moments

Before we begin ....

Let's just take a moment to reflect upon the hectic, pressured lives we lead. As teachers, we strive to be efficient and to meet our deadlines but our workload can seem so immense that we spend our days ticking off mental and written checklists, relentlessly aware of the demands of the world around us. We are watchful and attentive and constantly alert as we attempt to monitor, assess and meet our targets, engaged in a continual internal measurement of our own performance.

In all these activities our attention is directed outward towards our duties and responsibilities, and away from our own more personal needs. We give 'Golden Moments' to so many others in our lives that we may be losing our capacity to grasp and appreciate our own. We are vaguely conscious that we are in danger of losing something precious but we rush on. For so much of our lives we do what must be done but a Golden Moment is different.

When we grant ourselves a Golden Moment, however brief, we are choosing to replenish ourselves. We are rewarding ourselves so that, refreshed and energised, we can step back into the fray. You may need to be determined and creative about making space for yourself. Finding time when you ignore the clamour of demands can seem impossible and unacceptably self-indulgent but even brief moments of peace and receptivity can be very powerful. I am sharing a few of my own Golden Moments with you now because they work for me. I do this respectfully, aware that it may well be that not all of them will suit your particular circumstances. Just try them out and, if you like them, make them your own or adapt. Remember, you do a difficult job and you've earned the right to a few minutes 'out'!

Morning

Ground yourself

*B*efore you set off for work take the time to stand outside. Feel the crispness of the cold or the warmth of the sun on your skin. Simply enjoy the fresh air of the early morning. Look closely at one particular plant or tree and appreciate the intricate beauty of nature. Focus on the earth beneath your feet and imagine this energy rising up inside you. Allow a feeling of peace to enter you so that you can take it to school with you for the whole day.

Start the day positively

*P*repare the kitchen table the night before. Have ready a special brand of tea or coffee to drink and a treat to eat.

At breakfast, refuse to think about work and focus only on the aroma of your drink and consciously savour the taste of your food. Feel the heat of the cup in your hands; listen to the ticking of the clock or the familiar sounds of your house. A Golden Moment actively involves all your senses. Breathe slowly and let your senses help you to feel fully alive.

Sun-arise – early in the morning!

*B*e heroic; make the effort at least once a month to get up early when a fine day is forecast, just to watch the sun rise. Relax outside in a comfy chair in warm cosy clothes. Roll up your sleeves so that you can feel the quality of the air on your arms.

As you look at the dawn, observe the dark gradually giving way to light. Think about how amazing life is; feel the energy in the sun's rays. Concentrate on feeling this life force flow into your body. Feel the vibrancy of life and your appreciation of it as you leave for work.

Travelling

Holiday music

Select a piece of music that evokes a carefree holiday. Keep it in the car or on a Walkman and as you travel, relive the experiences in your mind. When life is becoming too hectic and stressful, slip this on to help you daydream. Try to recall the colours, sounds, scents and tastes of that holiday. Rekindle some of those positive, happy, carefree feelings. Be reassured that there are plenty more of those times ahead for you.

Get rid of that 'Bag of Contamination'

*T*he journey to and from school offers many chances for you to enjoy Golden Moments. Put any bags or boxes of schoolwork into the boot of your car or under your seat so that they do not sit next to you, contaminating your journey by reminding you of what you have not yet done and the piles of work you still have to do.

There's a world outside work

Stop if possible at a spot that allows you to look at nature for 5 minutes to enjoy the view. Breathe in the fresh air deeply and focus on a tiny fragment of beauty about you. Look at the way the light penetrates the leaves or the wind makes the grass move.

Quiet all voices in your mind; simply concentrate on the splendour of nature.

Back in the car work out a way you can weave into any of your lessons a feature of natural beauty for children to engage with.

During the day

Flash that smile!

Choose a recently taken, flattering photo that shows the laughing relaxed side of you. Glue it onto a piece of card. By the side of the photo write down the positive qualities people have mentioned to you. Keep it in your drawer or bag at school. When you are feeling low or negative about yourself, take out the photo and study it. Allow your mind to wander back to occasions when you felt truly alive. Allow these memories to balance your present negativity and reassure yourself that those good times will come again; the fun is inside you.

A golden notebook

*T*rawl through recent months and write down in a notebook all the positive comments about yourself that you have heard or that have been written down by family, friends or colleagues.

When you're feeling low in confidence, take out the notebook. Remind yourself that you are valued and that this low time is just an arid, dry period. Try to rekindle the warm glow you felt when the comments were given to you and allow this feeling to be stronger that any current self-doubt.

Put on the 'Golden Cloak'

*W*hen you arrive at school and take off down your coat to hang it up – imagine you take off the peg an armoured cloak of spun gold. Zip up the cloak and now you are protected! Hurtful words will just slide away without touching you but, magically, kind words can slip through to the inside making you feel warm and cosy. Practise this visualisation with children at the beginning of the day.

Be your own masseuse – anytime!

*G*ive yourself a hand massage, using a small phial of aromatherapy oils.

- Use the thumb of one hand to massage the palm, thumb and finger joints of the other hand.

- Press in small circles as firmly as you can.

- Pay attention to the 'web' between your forefinger and thumb, massaging this area as strongly as possible.

- Finish by pinching each finger, your two forefingers and thumb from the base, then the knuckle, then the tip.

- Now wiggle all your fingers and let them lie peacefully on your lap.

- Catch the scent of the oil and let your mind drift.

Reframe your thoughts

*A*ppreciate the value of what you do have. Be in the here and now. Life is too short for negativity.

Zip up the cloak and now you are protected! Hurtful words will just slide away without touching you but, magically, kind words can slip through to the inside making you feel warm and cosy. Practise this visualisation with children at the beginning of the day.

If you are feeling frustrated with the school buildings or lack of resources, close your eyes and think of all the positive aspects of your work place. Compare your situation with a far worse scenario.

Mentally, make a checklist of all the things that you **do** have e.g. warmth, weatherproof buildings, decent furnishings, safety, clean conditions, technical resources, some text books, etc. Emotionally – concentrate on one kindred spirit or the staff whose company you enjoy.

A special lunch

*H*aving prepared yourself a special lunch the night before, find somewhere quiet so you can take time to savour it, chewing slowly every mouthful.

Enjoy this self-indulgence at least once a week. You can also arrange to do this with colleagues who bring in special dishes so the menu will have the additional element of surprise.

Remember to drink plenty of water every day to keep your energy levels up. As you drink the water, feel the coolness, imagine it cleansing your body, revitalising your skin and giving you energy.

Break the pattern

*I*f you possibly can, take a brief walk outside the school to break the intensity of the day. Imagine, as you leave the gates, you put all your stress and worry into a plastic bag which you drop into a dustbin on your way out.

Now your mind is free to concentrate on the physical responses of your body. Walk briskly and if possible swing your arms. Focus on breathing through your nose and out through your mouth. Feel the legs stretching and your heart pumping. Enjoy your health.

A golden moment in the loo

Get together with colleagues to plan the decoration of the staff toilet!

Make it as luxurious as you possibly can with scented handwash, water face sprinkler, fluffy towels and vibrant colours. Put in a cassette player with a selection of relaxing tapes.

As you wash your hands, imagine that you are rinsing away all the irritations of the day and walk out feeling fresh.

Sometimes, in busy schools, going to the loo is the only break you get – so you may as well make it a good one!

Smile (or grit the teeth elegantly!)

*F*riendliness is catching so let others catch your beam and pass it on!
Make the effort to smile as you go into the staffroom. Before entering feel the smile deep inside you – make your eyes sparkle and your teeth gleam!

When they've gone....

*K*now that you've had a more positive influence than you often realise. When the children have gone home, don't rush out of the classroom immediately. Close the door, put on soothing music, sit back in your chair and savour the calm and quiet of the empty room for at least five minutes.

Think about the quiet children you've worked with today. Focus on several good moments that occurred. Maybe a child made you laugh, maybe a child tried hard today.

Back home

Stop before you start again

*W*hen you get home, sit quietly for five minutes to enjoy absolute peace and calm. Sit or lie peacefully and, starting from your toes, clench and unclench each part of your body so that you are thoroughly relaxed.

When you reach your head and you have screwed up your face and then relaxed it, imagine you are melting into the chair or bed.

Sun yourself now!

*F*ind a comfortable chair. Sit down and close your eyes. Imagine that you are in a pool of sunlight. Feel the warmth of the sun on your face as you relax your body.

You decide that through an effort of will you are going to pull the rays of sun in through your scalp. Feel a tingling sensation in your scalp as the sunlight tingles into your forehead and the warm glow enters your forehead.

Be conscious of your wrinkles melting away and your jaw relaxing. As the light moves slowly down through your body, feel the knots and tensions dissolve and melt away.

When you decide to return to the mainstream of life, think of something to concentrate on; the feel of the floor beneath your feet or the chair supporting your body. Open your eyes, stand up, stretch and remember the positive gift of life.

Be a secret dancer

*P*lay loud music, kick off your shoes and dance as madly and energetically as you can. Get lost in the rhythm and beat of the music. Sing along with the words until you feel thoroughly enlivened.

Golden Road – a creative visualisation

*C*lose your eyes and imagine that you are standing on a road that stretches before you into the distance. You may feel weary, but as you journey along the road you will receive sustenance and energy from different sources. For example, the warmth of the sun on your face, encouragement from friends and family, energising drink and food, the euphoria from a personal success you have had, the love of someone close.

Choose about half a dozen sources to visualise that will create in you the energy, confidence and certainty that you can reach the end of the road.

Golden Bubble – a creative visualisation

*C*lose your eyes and imagine that you are inside Golden Bubble. Visualise the glittering walls of the bubble cocooning and protecting you from the world outside. Imagine that your body is weightless and floating around inside the bubble. Let the feeling of lightness, well being and safety permeate every part of your mind and body.

Borrow animal calm

*F*or those of you that have a pet, spend five to ten minutes stroking it!
Allow your senses to become fully engaged in the task. Concentrate on the colour and texture of the animal's coat, its smell and feel. Let this time provide a sensual pleasure for you as you block out all other thoughts.

Collect together special writings

*B*rowse through your favourite poems or pieces of writing. Read slowly and allow yourself to enter fully into the thought or image.

Appreciate the writer's wisdom, humour or artistry. Consider that some of the young people you teach may go on to weave words together in a new and original way and some, like you, will appreciate the creativity of others.

Go for it

During the day, choose a piece of music that is guaranteed to make you feel buoyant and happy. Sing at the top of your voice, sway with the rhythm. Feel the energy.

Don't forget that outside school there is a world of music, concerts, festivals and creativity for you to enjoy.

Be daft — sing a few songs with the pupils during the day — your class will remember you forever!

Later that evening....

*C*hoose a physical task, such as slicing vegetables or watering the plants. Focus intently on the sight, touch and smell involved. Don't allow your mind to wander from the job in hand; instead allow your senses to become totally immersed in the task.

Bathe the day away

Sink into a deep bath with aromatherapy oils. Add to the ambience with candles and soothing music. Lie back, close your eyes and savour the relaxing experience.

Make sure you have a large fluffy towel ready for when you get out. Once you are wrapped up warmly, pull the plug out and imagine that all the stress of the day is draining away. Put a dab of lavender oil on your pillow to aid sleep.

Bed daydream – a creative visualisation

Lie on your bed in your most relaxed position and close your eyes. Imagine the sky filled with soft white cumulus clouds.

Think of each cloud floating down beside you and, one by one, place all your worries and anxieties of the day onto the cloud. Then watch, as it drifts away taking your cares with it.

Feel a sense of peace and lightness entering your body as each cloud disappears…sleep well.

A Final Thought

..or I bet you had no idea how a Golden Moment is scientifically validated!

*J*ust for a moment, think of that famous butterfly that flapped its wings somewhere far away in the rainforest and caused a hurricane. The butterfly wasn't the beginning of the story; it represents the pivotal moment when all the various possibilities for the future which existed at that moment were irrevocably pared down to a single outcome. That butterfly represents what scientists call a 'tipping point'.

Now think about your own life. As you rush from one situation to the next you are encountering tipping points throughout the day which change how you deal with the events that follow. You need to ensure that your tipping points are beneficial. If you take the time to have Golden Moments you are teaching your brain how to rest. Then your sympathetic nervous system activity decreases and your metabolism slows down. Your heart rate, blood pressure and breathing rates will fall and your brain's own electrical activity will change because, instead of supporting a maelstrom of signals, large numbers of its neurons will begin to fire in a pleasing synchrony. Taking a Golden Moment away from the stress of the day also activates the pleasure neurotransmitters in your brain and gives it a quick fix of dopamine, seratonin and oxytocin all of which make us feel good. Hmmm !!

Make a Golden Moment the tipping point of your day.

A Thought for the Day

A Thought for the Day

*I*f your day is really hectic and a golden moment is hard to find, don't forget that a positive thought is something that you can carry with you wherever you go, costs nothing and can be used to calm and re-energise yourself on even the busiest day! Choose which one you want to reflect on and return to it whenever you have a second to spare. You will soon find that even a snatched idea can change the "feel" of your day. Here are a few of my favourites:

The rhythm of your breathing becomes the rhythm of your day.

God grant me the serenity to accept the things that I cannot change, the courage to change the things that I can, and the wisdom to know the difference."

(Reinhold Niebuhr)

Sit in reverie and watch the changing colour of the waves that break upon the idle seashore of the mind.

(Henry Wadsworth Longfellow)

Worry doesn't drain tomorrow of its tension. It drains today of its strength.

(Anon)

"Too much of a good thing is wonderful."

(Mae West)

You can either be the candle or the mirror that reflects it.

(Anon)

"And all people live, not by reason of any care they have for themselves, but by the love for them that is in other people"

(Tolstoy)

"A vision without action is just a dream
Action without vision just passes the time
A vision with Action can change the world"

(Nelson Mandela)